A NO NONSENSE

100
Business Letters
and Memos

Steven Frank

LONGMEADOW
PRESS

Cover design by Kelvin P. Oden

Interior design by Richard Oriolo

Library of Congress Cataloging-In-Publication Data

Frank, Steven.
100 business letters and memos / Steven Frank. – 1st ed.
p. cm.
ISBN 0-681-41794-3 : $4.95
1. Commercial correspondence–Handbooks, manuals, etc.
I. Title. II. Title One hundred business letters and memos.
HF5726.F73 1993
651.7'5–dc20   93-23665
                                                             CIP

ISBN: 0-681-41794-3

Printed in United States

First Edition

0 9 8 7 6 5 4 3 2 1

CONTENTS

INTRODUCTION:
BUSINESS LETTER
BASICS

Letter writing has always played an important role in the world of business and has many advantages over other forms of communication. Unlike telephone conversations and meetings, the business letter ensures that both parties clearly understand whatever has been communicated and provides a permanent record for future reference. Moreover, when composing a letter, the writer may take the time to plan what he or she wants to say and then evaluate and adapt the letter to make certain that it clearly conveys the intended meaning.

Letters are used in business for a multitude of purposes, from setting up appointments to following up conversations and meetings, from providing important information to soliciting it. It's pretty safe to say that it would be difficult, perhaps impossible, to run a successful business without the use of carefully composed business letters.

This book includes over one hundred sample letters and memos that might be used by a small business, enabling you to choose the letter that fits your need. The letters in this book demonstrate what typical business letters look and sound like, providing models for business letters you might write yourself. Simply fill in whatever specific information is necessary where the words in the form are italicized.

With that in mind, this introduction will outline some of the basics of writing business letters—and you'll see how these principles have been put to use in the sample letters that follow.

I. FORMAT

Business letters should always be typed, single spaced, on one side of a piece of paper. Use either letterhead stationery or unlined paper of fine quality. The text should be centered on the page, with at least 1/2-inch margins on all sides. If you need to continue on to additional pages, type (*more*) at the bottom of the first page, and in the top left-hand corner of the next page, type *Page 2*, etc.

Business letters all follow a similar format, which includes the *return address* (of the writer of the letter), the *inside address* (of the person to whom the letter is sent, known as the *addressee*), as well as the *salutation* (greeting), the *body* of the letter, and the *closing* and *signature*. However, formats might differ in how they arrange and order these elements.

In the most common type of business letter, the name and address of the writer are centered at the top of the page. Everything else in the letter is typed flush left, beginning first with the date, followed by the inside address (the full name, title and address of the addressee), the salutation, the body of the letter, and the closing. You should skip a line between each one of these sections, and between paragraphs in the body of the letter.

In a less formal variation of this format, the return address, date, closing, and signature are aligned toward the right of the letter, while everything else remains flush left. In the least formal kind of letter, the return address, date, closing, and signature are aligned to the right, and the beginning of each paragraph in the body is indented five spaces.

The salutations will usually begin with *Dear*, followed by some form of address, usually the last name of the person to whom you are writing; it is always followed by a colon. Traditionally, the salutation includes either *Mr., Miss, Mrs.,* or *Ms.* Depending upon the gender and marital status of the addressee (i.e.—*Dear Mr. Smith:*). Today, this kind of differentiation is not as common. People often use *Ms.* when addressing a woman, even if they know her marital status. There are also many people who no longer differentiate based on gender and instead address the letter to the full name of the addressee (i.e.—*Dear Sue Smith:*).

If you do not know the name of the person to whom you are writing, you can write either *Dear Sir or Madam, To Whom It May Concern,* or use the name of the entire company (i.e.—*Dear Business Inc.:*)

There are several options for the closing of the letter. The most commonly used closings are *Sincerely,* or *Sincerely yours,* which are the most formal. Others include *Truly, Truly yours,* and *Very truly yours,* and *Best wishes,* which are all less formal and more personal. Only the first word in the closing is capitalized. Decide which closing to use, based upon how well you know the addressee and the purpose of the letter. For example, if you have a long-standing business relationship with someone and have become well acquainted with him or her, you might choose to write *Truly yours.* Similarly, if you are writing the letter for a special reason, such as commemorating a noteworthy occasion or enclosing a gift, you might write *Best wishes.*

Beneath the closing, leave four lines for the signature, and then type the full name of the writer. If you want to include the writer's title, it should appear on the following line, beneath the name and not preceding it.

Occasionally, additional information is included in the space beneath the closing. Some of the notations you might use include:

cc:	This notation will be followed by a name or names of people who have received a copy of the letter.
enc.	This notation indicates that additional materials are enclosed with the letter.
XX:yy	The letters in this notation stand for people's initials.

The first two (or three) capitalized initials that precede the colon are those of the writer of the letter; the initials that follow the colon, not capitalized, are those of the person who typed the letter.

SAMPLE FORMATS—Standard, Formal Business Letter
(on letterhead)

                    NAME OF WRITER
                    Company Name
                    Return Address
                    Return Address

DATE

NAME OF ADDRESSEE
TITLE OF ADDRESSEE
INSIDE ADDRESS
INSIDE ADDRESS

DEAR ADDRESSEE:

XXXXXXXXXXXXXXXXXXXXXXXXXXXXXXXXXXXXXXX
XXXXXXXXXXXXXXXXXXXXXXXXXXXXXXXXXXXXXXX
XXXXXXXXXXXXXXXXXXXXXXXXXXXXXXXXXXXXXXX
XXXXXXXXXXXXXX .

XXXXXXXXXXXXXXXXXXXXXXXXXXXXXXXXXXXXXXX
XXXXXXXXXXXXXXXXXXXXXXXXXXXXXXXXXXXXXXX
XXXXXXXXXXXXXXXXXXXXXXXXXXXXX .

XXXXXXXXXXXXXXXXXXXXXXXXXXXXXXXXXXXXXXX
XXXXXXXXXXXXXXXXXXXXXXXXXXXXXXXXXXXX .

XXXXXXXXXXXXXX .

CLOSING,

WRITER'S SIGNATURE
NAME OF WRITER
TITLE OF WRITER

NAME OF WRITER
Company Name
Return Address
Return Address

DATE

NAME OF ADDRESSEE
TITLE OF ADDRESSEE
INSIDE ADDRESS
INSIDE ADDRESS

DEAR ADDRESSEE:

XXXXXXXXXXXXXXXXXXXXXXXXXXXXXXXXXXXXXXX
XXXXXXXXXXXXXXXXXXXXXXXXXXXXXXXXXXXXXXX
XXXXXXXXXXXXXXXXXXXXXXXXXXXXXXXX.

XXXXXXXXXXXXXXXXXXXXXXXXXXXXXXXXXXXXXXX
XXXXXXXXXXXXXXXXXXXX.

XXXXXXXXXXXXXXX.

CLOSING,

WRITER SIGNATURE
NAME OF WRITER
TITLE OF WRITER

```
                                        NAME OF WRITER
                                        Company Name
                                        Return Address
                                        Return Address

                                        DATE

NAME OF ADDRESSEE
TITLE OF ADDRESSEE
INSIDE ADDRESS
INSIDE ADDRESS

DEAR ADDRESSEE:

      XXXXXXXXXXXXXXXXXXXXXXXXXXXXXXX
XXXXXXXXXXXXXXXXXXXXXXXXXXXXXXXXXXXXXX
XXXXXXXXXXXXXXXXXXXXXXXXXXXXXX.

      XXXXXXXXXXXXXXXXXXXXXXXXXXXXXXX
XXXXXXXXXXXXXXXXXXXX.

      XXXXXXXXXXXXX.

                                        CLOSING,


                                        WRITER SIGNATURE
                                        NAME OF WRITER
                                        TITLE OF WRITER
```

II. CONTENT AND STYLE

The business world is a busy, complicated place. That's why the most important part of writing business letters is that they convey your intended meaning quickly, concisely, and clearly. To help facilitate your letter writing, keep these guidelines in mind:

(1) **Keep to the point.** Business people rarely have the time to sit down and read a lengthy, complicated letter. Moreover, they might become turned off by a long letter and choose to ignore it, which can be particularly damaging when you are trying to solicit new business. You should therefore keep the letter as direct and simple as possible. Include only information that is necessary for conveying your intention, and use simple, straightforward language that sticks to the point at hand.

(2) **Spell out your purpose.** To further facilitate communication between you and your reader, you should always make it very clear exactly why you are writing, preferably in the first few lines of the letter. That way the addressee will immediately be made aware of the purpose and content of the letter and see why it is necessary for him or her to continue to read.

(3) **Be specific.** You should try to direct a letter specifically to the addressee as much as possible. This will help these letters seem more important and less like prefabricated form letters. Try to refer to the company and addressee by name in the body of the letter. Also try to include as much relevant, specific information as possible. For example, if you are referring to past correspondences, you might include the dates, or if you are referring to amounts of money (on invoices, checks, etc.), try to include the exact amounts.

(4) **Include some kind of closing.** The last few lines should bring the letter to some kind of close. You might recap the main points of the letter, indicate what you see as the next steps in your dealings, give your phone number for future contact, extend an invitation to provide more information, or thank the addressee for his or her attention.

(5) Gauge the tone. Your exact tone will depend both on how well you know the addressee and the purpose of your letter. Generally, you want to sound as serious and businesslike as possible, without becoming so formal as to seem stiff and remote. At the same time, you don't want to be too casual or colloquial, detracting from the magnitude and importance of your letter. Usually, a direct and straightforward tone is the most effective way of writing. Be careful to avoid becoming angry or insulting, even if you have a serious problem with the addressee. Maintain your cool, even in your writing. If you do know the person well and are writing for a lighter purpose (such as wishing a happy birthday or sending a gift), you might add more personal touches to the letter. Reading the sample letters that follow will give you a good sense of how to gauge the tone of your letter to suit your specific purpose.

A NOTE ON HOW TO USE THIS BOOK

Rather than providing a series of "fill in the blank" form letters, this book presents "real" letters used by a fictitious company called *Lost Your Marbles Toys & Games.* On the following pages, you'll find a series of letters involving many kinds of business interactions between *Lost Your Marbles* and its customers, suppliers, and employees that can serve as models for letters you might use yourself. By featuring "real letters" that include specific and detailed information, this book provides realistic samples, giving you a more accurate sense of how a particular letter will sound to the addressees.

In the sample letters and memos that follow, all specific information that differs from company to company has been highlighted. In order for you to adapt these letters to your own purposes, you merely need to fill in the relevant information in these highlighted areas. Please be aware that some of the letters might require a bit of additional altering in order to fit in with your own company's specifications.

I.
FOSTERING NEW
BUSINESS

NOTICE OPENING NEW BUSINESS

Dear Local Business:

I am pleased to announce that *LOST YOUR MARBLES TOYS &
GAMES* is now in business. Unlike most other *toy manufacturers* today, we are dedicated to making *toys and games* of only the highest
quality. All of our products are custom made, and we use only the
best materials available. We have also strived to develop a product
line featuring innovative and unique items that are certain to become
top sellers.

We are pledged to providing the most prompt and efficient services
available. As we are a relatively small company, we can devote individual attention to each one of our customers, insuring that their
needs and expectations are always met. We also offer special services
for our customers, such as *individualized payment plans, credit accounts,
and overnight delivery.*

We'd love to have you stop in and see what we're all about. Our
company is located at *888 Bleecker Street, New York, NY 12345.* If
you're interested in paying us a visit, just call my office and make an
appointment to come by. You can tour our facilities and see some of
the exciting new products we are working on.

If you'd like to hear more about *LOST YOUR MARBLES TOYS &
GAMES,* please feel free to call me at *212-555-1234.*

Sincerely yours,

Graham Peters
President
LOST YOUR MARBLES TOYS & GAMES

NEW BUSINESS PITCH LETTER

Ms. Cyndi Client
President and Chief Executive Officer
CYNDI'S HUGGABLES & LOVABLES, INC.
444 Greene Street
New York, NY 12345

Dear *Ms. Client*:

As the president of *a toy manufacturing company*, I am very well aware of the distinguished reputation of *CYNDI'S HUGGABLES & LOVABLES, INC.* In everything I have seen and heard about your company, I have been greatly impressed by the unparalleled dedication and innovation you have demonstrated that has obviously led to your current success.

Like *CYNDI'S HUGGABLES & LOVABLES, INC.*, we are also a unique company. Unlike most other *toy manufacturers*, we are devoted to making innovative *toys and games* of only the highest quality. All of our products are custom made, and we use only the best materials available. We have also worked to develop an unusual product line that I'm certain would make an excellent addition to the items you already offer.

Finally, as we are a relatively small company, we can devote individual attention to each one of our customers, insuring that their needs and expectations are always met

I'd like the opportunity to tell you more about *LOST YOUR MARBLES TOYS & GAMES* and to show you some of the exciting new products we have developed. I'll call sometime next week to set up a meeting.

Congratulations on your many accomplishments. I look forward to meeting you.

Sincerely yours,

Graham Peters
President
LOST YOUR MARBLES TOYS & GAMES

FOLLOW UP TO NEW BUSINESS MEETING

Ms. Cyndi Client
President and Chief Executive Officer
CYNDI'S HUGGABLES & LOVABLES, INC.
444 Greene Street
New York, NY 12345

Dear *Ms. Client*:

Thank you for meeting with me the other day. I enjoyed the opportunity to tell you more about *LOST YOUR MARBLES TOYS & GAMES*.

I hope you were able to get a sense of just how unique we are. I honestly believe our products are some of the most innovative and exciting ones available. Moreover, I think our commitment to prompt and efficient services is unparalleled.

I'd like to give you a *25% discount* on your first order from us, so that you might see firsthand everything that *LOST YOUR MARBLES TOYS & GAMES* has to offer. I guarantee that our products and services will meet your satisfaction. If they don't, your deposit will be refunded.

Remember that because we are a small company, you will receive individual attention from us that wouldn't be possible with some bigger manufacturers. I'll personally do all I can to insure you remain pleased with our products and services. If you ever want to discuss any questions, comments or problems you might have, you can always feel free to contact me directly.

It would truly be a pleasure to work for a company of your distinguished reputation. I hope you'll give us that opportunity.

Sincerely,

Graham Peters
President
LOST YOUR MARBLES TOYS & GAMES

RESPONSE TO
REQUEST FOR INFORMATION

Mr. Peter Prospect
JJ's EDUCATIONAL TOYS
333 Alameda Lane
Los Angeles, CA 12345

Dear *Mr. Prospect*:

Thank you for requesting information about *LOST YOUR MARBLES TOYS & GAMES*. Through the years, we have gained a reputation in the business community for producing innovative products and providing the most reliable services available. If you talk to any of our regular customers, you'll find that our items are frequently among the most popular.

I am enclosing our latest catalogue so that you can see the many *kinds of toys and games* we manufacture. For your convenience, there's a handy order form in the back that lists our prices and terms. We also accept telephone and fax orders, and the relevant numbers are included on the order form.

At *LOST YOUR MARBLES*, we make it a policy to do all we can to meet our customers' needs. For example, *should you request it, we can work out a special individualized payment plan for your orders. We also offer a credit policy for some of our regular customers, which entitles them to additional privileges.*

Please feel free to contact me should you have any questions about *LOST YOUR MARBLES TOYS & GAMES*. I hope you might become one of the many customers with whom we enjoy a long-standing and prosperous relationship.

Sincerely,

Graham Peters
President
LOST YOUR MARBLES TOYS & GAMES.
enc.

THANK YOU FOR ORDER/PROVIDE
MORE INFORMATION ON COMPANY

Ms. Allison Account
President
FUN & GAMES TIME
222 Main Street
New City, NY 12345

Dear *Ms. Account*:

Thank you for your recent order. It is already being processed and you can expect to receive our shipment by *the end of the month*. I'm certain you'll find everything to your satisfaction.

I am enclosing our most current catalogue so that you might see the many other unique products we manufacture and special services we provide. If you talk to any of our regular customers, I think you'll find that our products are frequently top-selling items. And with any order from *LOST YOUR MARBLES*, you can expect the same prompt and efficient services we pride ourselves upon.

I hope you will contact me should there be anything further my company might do to meet your needs or if you would like any more information about the products and services available from *LOST YOUR MARBLES TOYS & GAMES*.

Sincerely,

Graham Peters
President
LOST YOUR MARBLES TOYS & GAMES.
enc.

REQUEST INFO. TO BID ON PROJECT

Mr. Peter Prospect
JJ'S EDUCATIONAL TOOLS
333 Alameda Lane
Los Angeles, CA 12345

Dear *Mr. Prospect*:

Thank you for giving *LOST YOUR MARBLES TOYS & GAMES* the opportunity to bid on your project. We are currently putting together a proposal detailing the relevant costs, figures, and timetables.

In order for us to put together as comprehensive a proposal as possible, it would be extremely helpful for me to meet with you to find out more about your company. I would be happy to come out to visit your offices, as seeing your operation in person would also help me gain a better understanding of your company.

I'm sure you'll agree that such a meeting will help us to put together a proposal that will most suit your needs and expectations. I will call you later this week to try to set up an appointment.

I look forward to meeting with you and learning more about *JJ'S EDUCATIONAL TOYS*.

Sincerely,

Graham Peters
President
LOST YOUR MARBLES TOYS & GAMES.

Response To Invitation To Bid

Mr. Peter Prospect
JJ'S EDUCATIONAL TOYS
333 Alameda Lane
Los Angeles, CA 12345

Dear *Mr. Prospect*:

I am enclosing our proposal for your special project, which includes a detailed description of the terms by which we would agree to undertake this job. Please note that this includes a list of all costs and fees, as well as a timetable indicating when we would be able to begin and complete work.

I hope you'll understand that these prices and terms represent the best we have to offer. While the costs might be a bit more than other companies you might be considering, I can guarantee that we would provide the highest quality work available.

I sincerely hope you'll give us the opportunity to work on this project for *JJ'S EDUCATIONAL TOYS*

Sincerely,

Graham Peters
President
LOST YOUR MARBLES TOYS & GAMES.
enc.

II.
INTERVIEWING
AND HIRING

REQUEST TO INTERVIEW

Ms. Elyse Hopeful
888 High Ridge Lane
Happy Valley, NY 12345

Dear *Ms. Hopeful:*

After reviewing your resume, I find that your experience and skills are in keeping with what we are looking for in this position. I would therefore like the opportunity to meet with you in person.

Please contact my secretary to set up an appointment for an interview. I'd particularly like to hear what ideas and qualities you feel you can bring to *LOST YOUR MARBLES*. At that time, I can also tell you a bit more about the position and answer any questions you might have.

I look forward to meeting with you.

Sincerely,

Graham Peters
President
LOST YOUR MARBLES TOYS & GAMES.

REQUEST FOR SECOND INTERVIEW

Ms. Andrea Wannajob
444 Ridge Road
New Hills, NY 12345

Dear Ms. Wannajob:

Thank you for coming to our offices last week to interview for a position at *LOST YOUR MARBLES*. It was a pleasure meeting with you and getting to hear more about your qualifications. I found your professionalism and experience to be quite impressive.

At this time, I would like to invite you back for a second interview so that you might meet with some other key individuals on our staff. Also at that time, you will have an opportunity to tour our facilities and learn more about the specific responsibilities of the job. Shortly after this meeting, we will be prepared to make a final decision.

Please telephone my office to set up an appointment for the second interview. I look forward to this opportunity to talk with you further.

Sincerely,

Graham Peters
President
LOST YOUR MARBLES TOYS & GAMES.

No Positions Available

Mr. Job Hunt
1111 First Ave.
New York, NY 12345

Dear *Mr. Hunt*:

I recently received your resume and cover letter inquiring about openings at *LOST YOUR MARBLES TOYS & GAMES*. Your background is certainly impressive and you seem to hold many of the qualities and skills we look for in our employees.

Unfortunately, we have no positions available at the present time. However, I will keep your resume on file. Should there be an opening in the next few months, I will be happy to call you in for an interview.

Thank you for your interest in *LOST YOUR MARBLES*. I wish you the best of luck in your job search endeavors.

Sincerely,

Graham Peters
President
LOST YOUR MARBLES TOYS & GAMES.

NOTICE POSITION FILLED

Mr. Ned Nojob
222 96th Street
New York, NY 12345

Dear *Mr. Nojob*:

We recently received your resume and letter inquiring about the advertised opening at *LOST YOUR MARBLES TOYS & GAMES*. Unfortunately, that position has already been filled.

However, we were impressed by your background and experience and would like to keep your resume on file. Should another position become available in the next few months, we will be happy to call you in for an interview at that time.

Thank you for your interest in *LOST YOUR MARBLES TOYS & GAMES*. Best of luck in your job search endeavors.

Sincerely,

Graham Peters
President
LOST YOUR MARBLES TOYS & GAMES.

Notice Job Not Offered

Mr. Roger Reject
444 Fourth Avenue
New York, NY 12345

Dear Mr. Reject:

Thank you for coming in to interview last week. We all enjoyed the opportunity to meet you and talk further about your background and ideas.

As I told you during our meeting, we have been interviewing several applicants for this position. While we all thought your professionalism and much of your experience were quite impressive, we have found a candidate whose background and skills we believe are more suited to the position we have in mind.

However, I would like to keep your resume on file. Should another position become available in the next few months, I would be happy to call you in for another interview.

Again, thank you for your interest in our company. I congratulate you on your many accomplishments and wish you the best of luck in your job search endeavor.

Sincerely,

Graham Peters
President
LOST YOUR MARBLES TOYS & GAMES.

Notice Job Offered

Ms. *Ophelia Offer*
888 87th Street
New York, NY 12345

Dear *Ms. Offer*:

Thank you for coming in to our offices to interview *last week*. It was a pleasure meeting you and getting to talk to you further about your background and ideas.

After meeting with you and reviewing your resume, we are pleased to offer you a position at *LOST YOUR MARBLES TOYS & GAMES*. We thought your experience, skills, and personality were well-suited to the position and that you would be a valued addition to the *LOST YOUR MARBLES* team.

As we discussed in the interview, the opening is in the *art department* and carries the salary and responsibilities I described to you. I am enclosing a pamphlet with important information about our company's benefits package.

I would appreciate your informing me by the end of the week of your decision as to whether or not you accept the job. Should you accept the job, we would like you to begin work as soon as possible.

If you have any questions or require additional information in making your decision, please feel free to contact me directly.

Congratulations on all your achievements that have helped you reach this current success.

Sincerely,

Graham Peters
President
LOST YOUR MARBLES TOYS & GAMES.
enc.

RESPONSE TO JOB ACCEPTANCE

Ms. Ophelia Offer
888 87th Street
New York, NY 12345

Dear Ms. Offer:

I was delighted to hear of your decision to accept the position at
LOST YOUR MARBLES TOYS & GAMES. Everyone here joins me
in welcoming you. I think you'll find our company provides a unique
and exciting atmosphere in which to work.

As we had discussed, we expect you to begin work on *July 1*. At that
time, you will attend a brief orientation session with our personnel
director, who will inform you of our company policies and benefits.

Once again, welcome to *LOST YOUR MARBLES*. I look forward to
working with you.

Sincerely,

Graham Peters
President
LOST YOUR MARBLES TOYS & GAMES.

III.
CUSTOMER/
CLIENT
RELATIONS

APPRECIATION FOR YOUR BUSINESS

Ms. Cyndi Client
President and Chief Executive Officer
CYNDI'S HUGGABLES & LOVABLES, INC.
444 Greene Street
New York, NY 12345

Dear *Ms. Client*:

Thank you for your recent order. It is currently being processed and you can expect to receive your shipment *by the end of the month.*

I just want to take the time to let you know how much all of us at LOST YOUR MARBLES TOYS & GAMES appreciate your continued business. It is steady customers like you who enable us to continue providing special services as well as to expand our company with exciting new products.

As one of our valued customers, your concerns and opinions are important to us. I hope you'll contact me at any time to let me know if there is anything else we might be doing to better meet your needs.

Again, thank you for your business. I look forward to continuing our prosperous association in the days ahead.

Sincerely,

Graham Peters
President
LOST YOUR MARBLES GAMES & TOYS

SPECIAL OFFERS OR DISCOUNTS
(FOR SPECIAL CUSTOMERS)

Dear Valued Customer:

As one of *LOST YOUR MARBLES TOYS & GAMES'* steady customers, you are very important to us. To let you know just how much we appreciate your business, we'd like to offer you a special *20% discount* on your next order.

That's just our way of saying thank you for all your support. But if at any time there's anything I or anyone at our company might do to further improve our services for you, please do not hesitate to call.

Again, thank you for all your business and support.

Best wishes,

Graham Peters
President
LOST YOUR MARBLES TOYS & GAMES

NEW PRODUCT INFORMATION

Ms. Cyndi Client
President and Chief Executive Officer
CYNDI'S HUGGABLES & LOVABLES, INC.
444 Greene Street
New York, NY 12345

Dear *Ms. Client*:

We've got some exciting news and we want you to be one of the first to know. We're about to introduce an exceptional new product we've just created. The result of extensive planning and development, the new *Susan Sally Doll* is certain to be one of the most talked about *toy* items to be introduced this season.

As one of our steady customers, we want you to be one of the first to get a look at this exciting new item. You can expect to receive a complimentary sample in the mail in the next few weeks.

Additionally, we'll be giving valued customers like you a special opportunity to order this new product *one month* earlier than it will be made generally available—*at a special 20% discount*. You'll find a special order form enclosed with the sample.

We hope you are as enthusiastic about *Susan Sally* as we are. Please let us know what you think about it. Receiving comments and suggestions from our customers is one of the ways we are able to continue developing innovative products like this.

Best wishes,

Graham Peters
President
LOST YOUR MARBLES TOYS & GAMES

THANK YOU FOR
REFERRING BUSINESS TO US

Ms. Cyndi Client
CYNDI'S HUGGABLES & LOVABLES
444 Greene Street
New York, NY 12345

Dear *Ms. Client*:

I just want to thank you for referring *PETE'S SPORTS & TOYS* to *LOST YOUR MARBLES TOYS & GAMES*. We recently filled a substantial special order for them, and I believe they were quite pleased with it.

This kind of word of mouth is extremely important to us, as it is one of the primary ways in which we are able to expand our customer base. All of us at *LOST YOUR MARBLES* want to thank you for the kind words you put in for us.

I hope if there is anything I might do to return the favor, you won't hesitate to contact me. Again, thank you for your confidence in us and for your continued support.

Best wishes,

Graham Peters
President
LOST YOUR MARBLES TOYS & GAMES

THANK YOU FOR SPECIAL ORDER

Ms. Cyndi Client
President and Chief Executive Officer
CYNDI'S HUGGABLES & LOVABLES, INC.
444 Greene Street
New York, NY 12345

Dear *Ms. Client*:

It has come to my attention that *CYNDI'S HUGGABLES AND LOVABLES* recently placed a rather large special order. I am gratified to know that you consider our products worthy of this kind of substantial purchase.

I want to thank you for this order as well as for your continued business throughout the years. It is the support and encouragement of valued customers like you that has enabled us to continue expanding and improving our operation.

I also want to assure you the same care and efficiency will go into filling this order as you are accustomed to receiving for your regular orders. If you have any special needs or concerns, I hope you won't hesitate to call on me.

Again, thank you for all your business and support. It means a lot to us.

Best wishes,

Graham Peters
President
LOST YOUR MARBLES TOYS & GAMES

THANK YOU FOR
ATTENDING OUR EVENT

Ms. Cyndi Client
President and Chief Executive Officer
CYNDI'S HUGGABLES & LOVABLES
444 Greene Street
New York, NY 12345

Dear Ms. Client:

I just want to thank you for attending *our party in celebration of the opening of our new offices.* As always, it was nice to see you in person and to get the opportunity to talk face-to-face. It also meant a lot to all of us that our most valued customers were able to share in this special event.

The opportunity to speak in person with our customers is very valuable to us, as it enables us to gain a sense of how our customers perceive our work for them. I truly hope the dialogue we began the other night might continue in the future.

I look forward to sharing many other such special occasions with you.

Best wishes,

Graham Peters
President
LOST YOUR MARBLES TOYS & GAMES

REQUEST TO USE CLIENT FOR A REFERENCE

Ms. Cyndi Client
President and Chief Executive Officer
CYNDI'S HUGGABLES & LOVABLES, INC.
444 Greene Street
New York, NY 12345

Dear *Ms. Client*:

I am writing in the hope that you might grant us a small favor and permit us to refer prospective customers to you should they wish to contact one of our steady customers.

From our discussions together, I know that you have been pleased with the products and services you have received from *LOST YOUR MARBLES TOYS & GAMES*, and I also understand that you have recommended us to other stores on several occasions. I therefore thought you might consider allowing us to include you as one of our references in the future. Of course, I would only give out your name with your permission.

Please let me know if this would be acceptable to you. I sincerely appreciate your help with this, and I would, of course, be happy to reciprocate in a similar fashion.

Best wishes,

Graham Peters
President
LOST YOUR MARBLES TOYS & GAMES

REQUEST FOR TESTIMONIAL

Ms. Cyndi Client
President and Chief Executive Officer
CYNDI'S HUGGABLES & LOVABLES, INC.
444 Greene Street
New York, NY 12345

Dear *Ms. Client*:

Throughout the years, our two companies have enjoyed a healthy and prosperous business relationship. From our various meetings and conversations together, I know how pleased you have been with our products and services.

I therefore hope you might be willing to provide an endorsement to be used in our new promotional campaign. I would certainly be proud to have a company of your distinguished reputation standing behind us.

I sincerely hope you will grant us this request. Should you desire it, I would of course be happy somehow to return the favor.

Sincerely,

Graham Peters
President
LOST YOUR MARBLES TOYS & GAMES

LETTER OF SYMPATHY

Ms. Cyndi Client
President and Chief Executive Officer
CYNDI'S HUGGABLES & LOVABLES, INC.
444 Greene Street
New York, NY 12345

Dear *Ms. Client*:

I was greatly saddened to hear of your recent loss. All of us at *LOST YOUR MARBLES TOYS & GAMES* extend our deepest sympathy to you and your family. I hope it will provide you with some comfort to know that all of our thoughts are with you during this time of need.

Should there be anything I or any of us might do to help, I sincerely hope you will not hesitate to ask.

Truly yours,

Graham Peters
President
LOST YOUR MARBLES TOYS & GAMES

LETTER OF INTRODUCTION
FROM SALES REP. TO CUSTOMER

Ms. Cyndi Client
President and Chief Executive Officer
CYNDI'S HUGGABLES & LOVABLES, INC.
444 Greene Street
New York, NY 12345

Dear *Ms. Client*:

LOST YOUR MARBLES TOYS & GAMES has recently found it necessary to restructure the organization of its sales team. I'm delighted to say that I'll now be serving as your new sales representative.

I know that you have been working with another sales representative for some time. Let me assure you that the quality of service you receive from us will not be affected by these changes.

I'm enclosing my business card with my daytime and evening telephone numbers. Please feel free to contact me at any time should you need anything, have a question, or just want to talk.

Although I'll be coming to your offices in *the fall to show you our new product line*, I'd also like to set up a meeting just to say hello and to find out a bit more about your company's sales needs. I'll call sometime next week to set up an appointment.

I look forward to meeting you and to serving you in the coming months.

Sincerely,

Susie Sales
Sales Representative, Northeast Region
LOST YOUR MARBLES TOYS & GAMES
enc.

Sales Rep. To Client— Thank You For Meeting

Ms. Allison Client
ALLIE'S TOY SHOPPE
555 High Ridge Road
Portland, ME 54321

Dear *Ms. Client*:

I want to thank you for meeting with me *on Tuesday* to discuss *our new product line for the fall*. I'm certain you'll agree that we're offering some very unique products that are certain to become top-selling items.

I've already processed your initial order. You should expect to receive a shipment by *the end of the month*.

As your sales representative, it's my job to make certain you are aware of special offers like these and have ample opportunity to take advantage of them. *Let me point out that many of the new items I showed you are being offered at a discount for a limited time only.*

For your convenience, I've enclosed an additional order form and catalogue. I hope you'll take a look at the catalogue and take advantage of these low prices while they're still available.

You have my business card with my daytime and evening phone numbers. If you decide to order anything else, please feel free to contact me directly, and I'll be certain your order is processed quickly and efficiently.

Again, I enjoyed meeting with you, and I'll look forward to seeing you *in the spring*.

Sincerely,

Susie Sales
Sales Representative, Northeast Region
LOST YOUR MARBLES TOYS & GAMES
enc.

SALES REP. TO CLIENT—
FOLLOW-UP TO PROBLEM

Ms. Allison Client
ALLIE'S TOY SHOPPE
555 High Ridge Road
Portland, ME 54321

Dear *Ms. Client*:

I was glad to have the opportunity to meet with you last week and discuss your dissatisfaction with *LOST YOUR MARBLES TOYS & GAMES* in more detail. As your sales representative, it's my job to make certain that you are always pleased with our products and services. The information you provided will help me to take measures insuring that these problems do not recur.

I've already reported your complaint to our main offices, and the problems you described are being investigated. In the next few weeks, I think you'll find a definite improvement in our services. If not, please let me know and I'll make certain further action is taken.

Thank you for informing me of your opinion. It's only through feedback like this that we can make changes to keep our customers happy.

I'll speak to you soon to find out how everything is going.

Sincerely,

Susie Sales
Sales Representative, Northeast Region
LOST YOUR MARBLES TOYS & GAMES

APOLOGY FOR RETURNED PRODUCT

Ms. Cyndi Client
President and Chief Executive Officer
CYNDI'S HUGGABLES & LOVABLES, INC.
444 Greene Street
New York, NY 12345

Dear *Ms. Client*:

We recently received your returned shipment, and I regret that our product did not meet your expectations. Your account has already been credited for the amount.

We consider you a valued customer and your satisfaction is extremely important to us. I'd therefore like to offer you a *10% discount* on your next order so that you might give us another opportunity to demonstrate the quality work we provide for our customers.

I'm also enclosing our current catalogue so that you can see the many other products and services we make available to our customers. Perhaps we can provide you with something more suitable to your needs? We can also work together to manufacture something according to your exact specifications.

It always helps us to hear how we might better satisfy our customers. I would truly appreciate hearing any suggestions and comments from you about how we might better meet your expectations.

Sincerely,

Graham Peters
President
LOST YOUR MARBLES TOYS & GAMES
enc.

APOLOGY FOR DAMAGED PRODUCT

Ms. Cyndi Client
President and Chief Executive Officer
CYNDI'S HUGGABLES & LOVABLES, INC.
444 Greene Street
New York, NY 12345

Dear *Ms. Client*:

I understand that part of the last shipment you received from us arrived damaged. As you know, our materials are somewhat delicate, and, although we take extra precautions in our packaging, the products are occasionally damaged in the shipping and delivery process.

We can rush you replacements for the damaged items or, if you prefer, credit your account for the amount. Additionally, I would like to offer you a *10% discount* for the entire order as my way of apologizing for the inconvenience to you and demonstrating our appreciation for your business.

You are one of our valued customers and your satisfaction is our utmost concern. I hope you will contact me should there ever be anything we might do to better meet your needs.

Truly yours,

Graham Peters
President
LOST YOUR MARBLES TOYS & GAMES

Apology For Inability
To Deliver Order On Time

Ms. Cyndi Client
President and Chief Executive Officer
CYNDI'S HUGGABLES & LOVABLES, INC.
444 Greene Street
New York, NY 12345

Dear *Ms. Client*:

Due to a delay in the delivery of our supplies, your recent order is unfortunately not yet available for delivery.

I'm certain that as someone who also runs a business, you understand that these kinds of problems arise from time to time without notice. However, I assure you that we are doing everything we can to resolve this situation. As soon as we are able to complete your order, we will insure you get it as soon as possible.

In the meantime, if there is anything we might do to make it up to you, such as providing an alternate product or refunding your deposit, please let me know.

I apologize for any inconvenience this may cause you. Thank you for your understanding in this matter.

Sincerely,

Graham Peters
President
LOST YOUR MARBLES TOYS & GAMES

ACKNOWLEDGE RECEIPT
OF YOUR COMPLAINT

Ms. Cyndi Client
President and Chief Executive Officer
CYNDI'S HUGGABLES & LOVABLES, INC.
444 Greene Street
New York, NY 12345

Dear *Ms. Client*:

I recently received your letter of complaint about our services, and I sincerely regret that we have not been meeting your expectations.

At *LOST YOUR MARBLES TOYS & GAMES*, our customers' opinions are extremely important to us. I personally assure you that your complaint is being given careful consideration. Should we need any additional information from you regarding the problem, I will contact you directly.

I hope you will give us the opportunity to demonstrate how efficiently we respond to our customers' comments. I think you'll find a marked difference in our services in the future. In the meantime, I apologize for any inconvenience this may have caused you.

Sincerely,

Graham Peters
President
LOST YOUR MARBLES TOYS & GAMES

FOLLOW-UP LETTER TO COMPLAINT

Ms. Cyndi Client
President and Chief Executive Officer
CYNDI'S HUGGABLES & LOVABLES, INC.
444 Greene Street
New York, NY 12345

Dear *Ms. Client*:

I wanted to let you know that, as promised, I have looked into the situation you described in your letter of complaint *dated May 15*. As a result of your comments and my inquiry, measures have been taken to insure that this problem will not recur.

I sincerely appreciate your taking the time to notify us of this problem. As you know, we pride ourselves on providing quality products and efficient service to our customers. As a result of your comments, we were able to make improvements enabling us to serve our customers even more productively.

I hope you will give us the opportunity to show you how we can now better meet your needs. Thank you again for your letter and for your understanding in this matter.

Sincerely,

Graham Peters
President
LOST YOUR MARBLES TOYS & GIFTS

SUDDEN DROP IN BUSINESS

Mr. John Customer
JINGLE SPORTING GOODS
333 Wall Street
New Haven, CT 23451

Dear *Mr. Customer*:

In going over our records, I noticed that while you had consistently been placing substantial orders with us, your business seems to have dropped in recent months. I'm surprised to find this because, as far as I know, you have been pleased with our products and services in the past.

I hope this change is not due to your dissatisfaction with our work or services. However, if this is the case, I truly hope you will let me know what the problem is and give me the opportunity somehow to make amends. I've found that the feedback I've received from customers has enabled me to make substantial improvements in our company.

I would greatly appreciate hearing from you in regard to this matter.

Sincerely,

Graham Peters
President
LOST YOUR MARBLES TOYS & GAMES

IV.
FINANCIAL
DEALINGS WITH
CUSTOMERS
AND CLIENTS:
CREDIT
AND BILLING

INFO ON CREDIT TERMS

Ms. Cyndi Client
President and Chief Executive Officer
CYNDI'S HUGGABLES & LOVABLES, INC.
444 Greene Street
New York, NY 12345

Dear *Ms. Client:*

Thank you for your interest in establishing credit with *LOST YOUR MARBLES TOYS & GAMES.* In brief, we generally offer credit *for up to $30,000,* and our usual terms are *net due in 30 days, with a 15% finance charge on balances past due per month.*

I am enclosing a brochure with more detailed information about our company's credit policy as well as a credit application. Once we receive your completed application, our accounting department will review it and, if everything is in order, will establish an account for your company.

If you have any questions about our company or the credit application, please do not hesitate to contact me directly. Again, thank you for your interest in *LOST YOUR MARBLES TOYS & GAMES.* I hope this might be the beginning of a long and prosperous business relationship between us.

Sincerely,

Graham Peters
President
LOST YOUR MARBLES TOYS & GAMES

enc.

EXTEND CREDIT TO CUSTOMER

Ms. Cyndi Client
President and Chief Executive Officer
CYNDI'S HUGGABLES & LOVABLES, INC.
444 Greene Street
New York, NY 12345

Dear Ms. Client:

After reviewing your application, we are pleased to extend credit to *CYNDI'S HUGGABLES & LOVABLES, INC.*

I am enclosing a pamphlet detailing the specifics of our credit terms and billing schedule. In general, our bills are sent out *on the first of each month and are due within 30 days.* You do not have to pay any finance charges provided that payment is made within the *30-day grace period.*

Although we usually request payment in full, we can also establish an individualized payment plan to suit your company's needs. If you are interested in doing so, please contact the accounting department for more information.

As one of our credit accounts, we consider you one of our most important and valued customers. Should there be anything special we can be doing for you, please let us know.

May this be the start of a prosperous association between our two companies.

Sincerely,

Graham Peters
President
LOST YOUR MARBLES TOYS & GAMES
enc.

TURN DOWN OF CREDIT APPLICATION

Mr. Reginald Client
President
REGGIE'S CUTE & FUN STUFF, INC.
999 Greene Street
New York, NY 12345

Dear *Mr. Client*:

Thank you for your recent application for credit with *LOST YOUR MARBLES TOYS & GAMES*. After reviewing your application, our accounting department determined we will unfortunately not be able to extend credit to you at this time.

We make a policy of only offering credit to those customers with whom we have a long-standing business relationship or who have an extensive credit history. In reviewing your application, our accounting department felt that there was not enough of a credit history for us to base a decision at the present time. However, we still consider you a valued customer and would certainly reconsider your application some time in the near future.

In the meantime, I invite you to take advantage of the many discounts and special offers we provide our steady customers. I'll be certain to inform you of these opportunities whenever they come up.

Sincerely,

Graham Peters
President
LOST YOUR MARBLES TOYS & GAMES

STOP CREDIT ACCOUNTS DUE
TO DELINQUENT PAYMENTS

Mr. John Customer
JINGLE SPORTING GOODS
333 Wall Street
New Haven, CT 12345

Dear Mr. Customer:

When our company extended credit to you, we did so with the understanding that you would make payments as promptly as possible. According to our records, you currently have an outstanding balance of $4,250.15. Moreover, you have consistently been delinquent in making your payments.

As a small company, we rely on receiving regular payments from our customers in order to cover our manufacturing and shipping costs. Obviously, we cannot afford to provide these products and services on credit unless we receive payment.

Unfortunately, that means we are going to have to deny you credit until you demonstrate an ability to make payments more responsibly. Until that time, I hope you will continue to use our company. We still value your business and would be happy to fill your orders on a C.O.D. basis.

Please contact me should you have any questions regarding this matter.

Sincerely,

Graham Peters
President
LOST YOUR MARBLES TOYS & GAMES

WILL FILL ORDER DESPITE DELINQUENT ACCOUNT

Ms. Cyndi Client
President and Chief Executive Officer
CYNDI'S HUGGABLES & LOVABLES
444 Greene Street
New York, NY 12345

Dear *Ms. Client:*

This letter is to inform you that we received your recent order and that it is currently being processed. You can expect to receive your shipment by *the end of the month.*

According to our records, your account shows an outstanding balance of *$4,050.14.* Normally we would be unable to fill an order for a customer with such a large outstanding balance. However, as you are one of our most valued customers, I'm happy to make an exception and fill this order for you. I'm certain, though, that you'll settle your account with us as soon as possible.

As you know, we rely upon receiving prompt payment from our customers so that we may continue to manufacture products for them on a credit basis. Please settle your account so that we might continue to extend you these privileges.

Please feel free to telephone me should there be anything I can do to assist you in making your payment.

Sincerely,

Graham Peters
President
LOST YOUR MARBLES TOYS & GAMES

UNABLE TO PROCESS ORDER
DUE TO UNPAID BALANCE

Mr. John Customer
JINGLE SPORTING GOODS
333 Wall Street
New Haven, CT 12345

Dear *Mr. Customer*:

We recently received your order for *500 Bull's-Eye dart sets*. According to our records, you currently have an outstanding balance of $4,250.15 for previous orders. Unfortunately, until that balance is paid off, we simply cannot afford to process any more orders for you.

We greatly value your business and would like to continue to provide you with the quality products and services we have in the past. However, I'm certain you'll understand that we need to receive steady payments from our customers in order to cover the costs of manufacturing our products.

As soon as your balance is paid off, we will be happy to fill your next order. Please feel free to contact me should you have any questions regarding this matter.

Sincerely,

Graham Peters
President
LOST YOUR MARBLES TOYS & GAMES

NEED DEPOSIT TO PROCESS ORDER

Mr. John Customer
JINGLE SPORTING GOODS
333 Wall Street
New Haven, CT 12345

Dear Mr. Customer:

Thank you for your recent order for *10,000 Bull's-Eye dart sets*. According to company policy, we require a *50%* deposit before we can process large quantity orders such as this one. This deposit helps us cover some of the additional materials and manufacturing costs such a large order requires.

As soon as we receive payment of *50%* of your total balance, we will be happy to fill your order and ship it to you as promptly as possible.

Additionally, you might consider applying for credit with our company. Our credit customers receive various special offers and benefits, including a waiver of the deposit requirement.

Please feel free to telephone me should you have any questions.

Sincerely,

Graham Peters
President
LOST YOUR MARBLES TOYS & GAMES

Notice of Delinquent Payment
on Service Contract

Mr. Buck Barowner
BUCK'S BAR & TAVERN
111 Buffalo Road
Ithaca, NY 12345

Dear *Mr. Barowner*:

In going over our records, it has come to my attention that your service contract for the *Susan Sally pinball machine* has not been paid in 60 days.

As you know, in order for you to receive the service that your contract entitles you to, you must make the payments regularly. We have found that *pinball machines* frequently need servicing, which is why we recommend maintaining the service contract. It is in your best interest to make your payments as soon as possible, so that you might receive prompt service from us when the need arises.

Please feel free to contact me should you have any questions regarding your service contract.

Sincerely,

Graham Peters
President
LOST YOUR MARBLES TOYS & GAMES

WRONG AMOUNT RECEIVED
FROM CUSTOMER

Ms. Cyndi Client
President and Chief Executive Officer
CYNDI'S HUGGABLES & LOVABLES
444 Greene Street
New York, NY 12345

Dear *Ms. Client*:

Thank you for your recent check of *$5,000.00*. While we appreciate your prompt payment, the balance shown on your last invoice was in the amount of *$5,750.00*.

I understand that such oversights occasionally occur. If you pay the difference by the end of the week, we'll consider your balance paid in full and not carry over the difference to next month, when it would be susceptible to the *15%* finance charge for late payment.

Please feel free to contact me if you have any questions regarding the balance of your payment. Otherwise, I'll look forward to receiving a check this week.

Sincerely,

Graham Peters
President
LOST YOUR MARBLES TOYS & GAMES

RECEIPT OF DUPLICATE CHECK

Ms. Cyndi Client
President and Chief Executive Officer
CYNDI'S HUGGABLES & LOVABLES, INC.
444 Greene Street
New York, NY 12345

Dear *Ms. Client:*

We recently received a check from you in the amount of *$500.00.*
However, according to our records, we had already received payment
from you for that invoice *on April 1.*

I would be happy to return the check to you, or credit your account
for the amount on your next bill. Please let me know how you would
like us to proceed.

As always, we greatly appreciate the promptness and conscientiousness you demonstrate in making your monthly payments.

Sincerely,

Graham Peters
President
LOST YOUR MARBLES TOYS & GAMES

NOTICE CHECK RETURNED
FROM THE BANK

Mr. *John Customer*
JINGLE SPORTING GOODS
333 Wall Street
New Haven, CT 12345

Dear *Mr. Customer*:

Your bank, *The Money Institution*, recently returned your check to us, *in the amount of $4,250.15*, because of insufficient funds. I'm certain this error is merely due to a miscalculation or oversight. We would, however, like to receive that payment as soon as possible.

I am enclosing the returned check for your records. Please contact me should there be any problem.

Thank you for your immediate attention to this matter.

Sincerely,

Graham Peters
President
LOST YOUR MARBLES TOYS & GAMES

enc.

REMINDER NOTICE
—BILL 15 DAYS PAST DUE

Mr. Joe Storeowner
LE TOY STORE
555 Fifth Avenue
New York, NY 12345

Dear *Mr. Storeowner*:

This is just a quick reminder that your bill of last month, dated *April 1*, is due on *May 1*. As you know, according to our credit terms, you have *30 days to pay without a penalty, and past-due balances are subject to a finance charge of 15% per month*. I know you'll want to avoid accruing finance charges by paying your balance as soon as possible.

Prompt payment of your bills is greatly appreciated, as it enables us to continue to provide the quality products and efficient services our customers expect from us.

If you have already paid your bill, please disregard this letter. Feel free to contact me should you have any questions about your account.

Sincerely,

Graham Peters
President
LOST YOUR MARBLES TOYS & GAMES

UNPAID BILL
—FIRST NOTICE (30 DAYS PAST DUE)

Mr. Joe Storeowner
LE TOY STORE
555 Fifth Avenue
New York, NY 12345

Dear *Mr. Storeowner*:

In going over our records, I see that your bill, dated *April 1,* is still outstanding. That makes it over 30 days late and brings your current balance up to *$5,750.00,* including a finance charge for late payment. You may remember that our credit terms stipulate *payment is due within 30 days of billing, whereupon a 15% finance charge is added for each additional month.*

I'm certain this was just an oversight on your part and now that you have been made aware of the situation you will take action in settling your account. If you have already paid your bill, please disregard this letter.

Thank you in advance for your immediate attention to this matter. If I can be of any assistance, please feel free to contact me directly.

Sincerely,

Graham Peters
President
LOST YOUR MARBLES TOYS & GAMES

UNPAID BILL
—SECOND NOTICE (60 DAYS PAST DUE)

Mr. Joe Storeowner
LE TOY STORE
555 Fifth Avenue
New York, NY 12345

Dear Mr. *Storeowner*:

It has come to my attention that your bill, dated *April 1*, has still not been paid. That makes it over two months past due, and brings your total balance to *$6,612.50*, including finance charges.

Two months past due is excessively late and I'm certain you can see why it concerns me. At *LOST YOUR MARBLES TOYS & GAMES*, we pride ourselves on providing quality products quickly and efficiently to our customers. In order to do so, however, we rely on receiving prompt and steady payments from our customers.

Please send us a check today. It will save you additional finance charges, and enable us to maintain a healthy business relationship with you. If you're having trouble making your payment, contact me so that we can work out a plan to help you meet these payments.

Thank you in advance for your immediate attention to this matter. Let me know if there is anything I might do to help you expedite your payment.

Sincerely,

Graham Peters
President
LOST YOUR MARBLES TOYS & GAMES

Unpaid Bill
—Third Notice (90 Days Past Due)

Mr. Joe Storeowner
LE TOY STORE
555 Fifth Avenue
New York, NY 12345

Dear *Mr. Storeowner*:

I am concerned to find that while I have formally requested payment of your bill, dated *April 1,* it has still not been paid. That makes it over three months late, and brings your total balance up to *$7,604.38.* Furthermore, although I have repeatedly attempted to contact you by telephone and through the mail in order to discuss the situation, I have not received any reply.

It would really be in both of our best interests if you act expeditiously in this matter. As I am certain you are aware, a history of late payments can unfortunately have serious ramifications for your company's financial reputation. If we are called upon to provide a credit reference for you, I would like to be able to speak well of your company.

I sincerely hope we can settle this matter and continue our business relationship. Insure that your credit rating stays in good standing by making certain we receive your payment by the end of this week.

Sincerely,

Graham Peters
President
LOST YOUR MARBLES TOYS & GAMES

UNPAID BILL
—FOURTH NOTICE

Mr. Joe Storeowner
LE TOY STORE
555 Fifth Avenue
New York, NY 12345

Dear Mr. Storeowner:

I am greatly distressed to find that your bill of April 1 has still not been paid. It is imperative that you either make the payment immediately or attempt to contact me to discuss it.

I have written several times requesting that you pay your bill as soon as possible; I am now requiring that you pay by the end of this week, or I will be forced to notify my attorneys of this situation.

I look forward to receiving your check this week.

Sincerely,

Graham Peters
President
LOST YOUR MARBLES TOYS & GAMES

UNPAID BILL
—FIFTH AND FINAL NOTICE

Mr. Joe Storeowner
LE TOY STORE
555 Fifth Avenue
New York, NY 12345

Dear *Mr. Storeowner:*

Your bill of *April 1* is now well over three months late and totals
$8,745.04. Such excessive lateness is completely unacceptable. My
company obviously cannot afford to do business with a customer who
does not pay for our products and services.

I have written on several occasions requesting payment and have attempted to contact you by telephone, but I still have not received a
response. Unless I hear from you or receive payment by *August,* I am
therefore going to turn this matter over to my attorney. I hope that
will not be necessary and that you'll pay your balance right away.

Sincerely,

Graham Peters
President
LOST YOUR MARBLES TOYS & GAMES

UNPAID BILL
—THREAT TO CUT OFF CREDIT

Mr. Joe Storeowner
LE TOY STORE
555 Fifth Avenue
New York, NY 12345

Dear *Mr. Storeowner*:

When my company extended credit to you, we did so with the understanding that you would make every effort to pay your bills as promptly as possible. However, while we have continually delivered our products on time, you have consistently been delinquent in making your payments.

In order to continue to extend credit to you, I'm therefore going to have to ask you to pay off your balance, totaling *$8,745.04*, by the end of the week. Please do this right away so that we can continue extending this special service to you.

Please disregard this letter if you have already paid your balance. Feel free to contact me if you have any questions regarding this matter.

Sincerely,

Graham Peters
President
LOST YOUR MARBLES TOYS & GAMES

REQUEST FOR ACCOUNT
OF FINANCIAL HISTORY

Ms. Cyndi Client
President and Chief Executive Officer
CYNDI'S HUGGABLES & LOVABLES, INC.
444 Greene Street
New York, NY 12345

Dear *Ms. Client*:

We are currently in the process of updating our records. It would be of great help to us if you could provide a detailed account of your company's financial dealings with *LOST YOUR MARBLES TOYS & GAMES.*

I realize that this will require some time on your part. However, it will be extremely helpful to us in maintaining the efficient services we provide for you.

Thank you for your understanding and cooperation in this matter.

Sincerely,

Graham Peters
President
LOST YOUR MARBLES TOYS & GAMES

V.

FINANCIAL

DEALINGS WITH

SUPPLIERS,

VENDORS, AND

SERVICES

CONFIRMATION OF
AGREEMENT WITH SUPPLIER

Mr. Peter Paper
PETER'S PAPER PRODUCTS
444 Road Way
New York, NY 12345

Dear *Mr. Paper*:

I am writing to confirm the details of our agreement as we discussed it earlier today.

Per our arrangement:

(1) *You will deliver a quantity of 10 cartons of paper to our offices by the first of every month.*

(2) *We will be billed by you on a monthly basis. As long as we pay our bill within 30 days, we will not be subject to any penalty charges.*

(3) *You will notify us in writing 30 days prior to any price increases.*

(4) *Should we want to make a change in our order, we will notify you of the change two weeks prior to delivery.*

Assuming this agrees with your understanding of our agreement, I expect to receive our shipment on *the first of this month*. However, should you have any questions as to the details stipulated here, please respond in writing by the end of this week.

I look forward to a long and healthy association between our two companies.

Sincerely,

Graham Peters
President
LOST YOUR MARBLES TOYS & GAMES

FAILURE TO DELIVER SUPPLIES

Mr. Peter Paper
PETER'S PAPER PRODUCTS
444 Road Way
New York, NY 12345

Dear *Mr. Paper*:

Pursuant to our agreement, as outlined in my letter *of May 3*, you were to deliver our order by *the first of the month*. To date, we have not yet received this month's delivery, making our order *15 days* overdue.

As I emphasized to you when we first spoke, my company relies upon receiving our supplies on a regular basis. Your failure to deliver on time holds up our work, costing us great time and expense, and seriously affects our ability to satisfy our customers' needs. This is unacceptable and cannot continue.

Please see to this matter immediately. I trust I can rely upon you to insure that this problem will not recur in the future.

Sincerely,

Graham Peters
President
LOST YOUR MARBLES TOYS & GAMES

TERMINATION OF
ACCOUNT WITH SUPPLIER

Mr. Peter Paper
PETER'S PAPER PRODUCTS
444 Road Way
New York, NY 12345

Dear Mr. Paper:

Your company has consistently been delinquent in delivering our supplies. According to our initial agreement, you were to deliver my order by *the first of the month*, yet you failed to meet this due date on *three* occasions.

As I have informed you in my previous letters, this inefficiency is unacceptable. Since your failure to deliver in compliance with our written agreement has seriously jeopardized our ability to do business, I am terminating our account with you as of today.

Sincerely,

Graham Peters
President
LOST YOUR MARBLES TOYS & GAMES

REQUEST FOR CREDIT INFORMATION

Mr. Glenn Supplier
GLENN'S GLASSWARES
777 Hudson Street
Hoboken, NJ 12345

Dear *Mr. Supplier*:

For the past several months, my company has been purchasing *various glass products* from you on a regular basis and in large quantities. Your *glasswares* are key components in the manufacturing of our products and we plan on continuing to purchase materials through you.

I am now very much interested in establishing a credit account with *GLENN'S GLASSWARES*, as it would enable us to manufacture and stock more products for our customers and thereby expand our business.

If you look into our financial records or make inquiries in the business community, you'll find *LOST YOUR MARBLES TOYS & GAMES* has a solid reputation. We also maintain a healthy base of steady customers, insuring a constant influx of funds.

Please send me information regarding your company's credit policy and terms as soon as possible. I look forward to hearing from you.

Sincerely,

Graham Peters
President
LOST YOUR MARBLES TOYS & GAMES

REQUEST TO RETURN DEPOSIT

Mr. Stew Supplies
STEW'S PLASTICS
333 111th Street
Bronx, NY 12345

Dear *Mr. Supplies*:

In order for us to establish credit with *STEW'S PLASTICS*, you had requested a deposit in the amount of *$1,000.00* At that time, we were led to understand that the deposit would only be held until such a time as we had demonstrated a reliable payment record.

I think if you look over our account for the past year, you'll find that we have consistently made our payments to you in a prompt and efficient manner. We have certainly demonstrated our conscientiousness in terms of our financial dealings.

In light of this, we are requesting a refund of our initial deposit. Please send me a check as soon as possible.

Thank you for your attention to this matter.

Sincerely,

Graham Peters
President
LOST YOUR MARBLES TOYS & GAMES

APOLOGY FOR LATE
PAYMENT TO SUPPLIER

Mr. Sam Supplier
PRETTY PAPER GOODS, INC.
111 Mott Street
New York, NY 12345

Dear *Mr. Supplier*:

Enclosed please find our check in the amount of *$500.00* for your invoice dated *April 1*.

I realize that our payment is a bit late this month and I apologize for any inconvenience this may have caused. If you look at our payment record, I think you'll find that this kind of oversight rarely occurs. Given our history with you, I hope we'll remain in good standing with your company.

I sincerely appreciate your understanding in this matter. I assure you that I'll do all I can to insure this kind of oversight does not recur.

Truly yours,

Graham Peters
President
LOST YOUR MARBLES TOYS & GAMES

RESPONSE TO
OVERDUE PAYMENT LETTER

Mr. Sam Supplier
PRETTY PAPER INC.
111 Mott Street
New York, NY 12345

Dear *Mr. Supplier*:

We recently received a letter from you regarding late payment for an invoice dated *May 1*. However, according to our records, we never received an invoice from you for that order.

If you look into your own records, you'll see that we have consistently paid our bills on time. Moreover, *LOST YOUR MARBLES TOYS & GAMES* has a solid reputation in the local business community. Obviously, had we received an invoice from you, we would certainly have paid it in our usual prompt fashion.

When we receive an invoice from you, we will be happy to make our payment.

Sincerely,

Graham Peters
President
LOST YOUR MARBLES TOYS & GAMES

DUPLICATE INVOICE RECEIVED

Mr. Sam Supplier
PRETTY PAPER, INC.
111 Mott Street
New York, NY 12345

Dear *Mr. Supplier*:

We recently received a second invoice from you, *dated April 1,* in the amount of *$500.00.* However, according to our records, that amount has already been paid.

I am enclosing copies of the original invoice and our check. You can see that we made our payment on *April 15.* Please settle our account in your records.

Thank you for your attention to this matter.

Sincerely,

Graham Peters
President
LOST YOUR MARBLES TOYS & GAMES
enc.

Erroneous Late Fee Charged

Mr. Sam Supplier
PRETTY PAPER INC.
111 Mott Street
New York, NY 12345

Dear *Mr. Supplier*:

I noticed that on the last invoice we received from *PRETTY PAPER INC.*, we were erroneously charged a penalty for late payment of our balance from the preceding month. However, according to our records, we made that payment on *April 15*, within the 30-day grace period.

I am enclosing copies of the original invoice and our check, *dated April 15*. You can clearly see that our payment was made on time. Please adjust our account in your records.

I am also returning the invoice with the incorrect balance. We will be happy to pay our balance upon receipt of an invoice detailing the correct amount.

Thank you for your attention to this matter.

Sincerely,

Graham Peters
President
LOST YOUR MARBLES TOYS & GAMES
enc.

WRONG BILL FROM SUBCONTRACTOR

Mr. Carl Carpenter
CARL'S WOOD SHOP
222 5th Street
New York, NY 12345

Dear *Mr. Carpenter*:

We recently received a bill from you for your work. However, at the time we hired you for this project, we discussed making payment only when the job was completed to our satisfaction. As of today, the work is not yet finished.

I am therefore returning the invoice with this letter. Please send me another bill upon completion of the job. At that time, should the work meet with our satisfaction, we will be happy to pay you in full.

If you have any questions regarding this, feel free to contact my office.

Sincerely,

Graham Peters
President
LOST YOUR MARBLES TOYS & GAMES

RECEIPT OF WRONG PRODUCT
FROM SUPPLIER;
REQUEST REFUND OR CREDIT

Mr. Stew Supplies
STEW'S PLASTICS
333 111th Street
Bronx, NY 12345

Dear *Mr. Supplies*:

We recently received an order from *STEW'S PLASTICS* that included a different item than the one we requested. I'm enclosing a copy of our order form. You can see that we clearly requested a quantity of *#7 plastic knobs*, and not *the #42 plastic rods* we received.

Those parts are crucial components in the manufacturing of our products. I therefore expect you to send us the correct order immediately or refund us the amount of our deposit.

Additionally, I need to know how you would like us to handle the return of your shipment. My company obviously should not have to pay for it. Do you want us to use our own delivery service and charge you for the return, or will you arrange to pick it up yourself? Please let me know how you would like us to proceed as soon as possible.

Thank you for your immediate attention to this matter.

Sincerely,

Graham Peters
President
LOST YOUR MARBLES TOYS & GAMES
enc.

TO SUPPLIER
—DISSATISFACTION WITH PRODUCT

Mr. Stew Supplies
STEW'S PLASTICS
333 111th Street
Bronx, NY 12345

Dear *Mr. Supplies*:

When I initially contacted you, I conveyed how important it is that we receive *plastic parts* of only the highest quality, as they are key components in the manufacturing of our *toys*. At that time, you assured me that you would supply only the best materials available. I was therefore dismayed to find that the recent shipment we received from you was not of the quality we were expecting.

The *plastic parts* you provided are not satisfactory to our needs. I am therefore returning your shipment to you and request an immediate refund for the entire amount plus the cost of the shipping.

Please contact *my head of production, Mr. Paul Production,* to discuss in more detail what we may expect from you. If you are unable to provide us with the parts we require, we will be forced to find a supplier more suitable to our needs.

Sincerely,

Graham Peters
President
LOST YOUR MARBLES TOYS & GAMES

Displeasure With Service

Mr. Saul Servicer
S&S MESSENGER SERVICE
999 Ninth Street
New York, NY 12345

Dear *Mr. Servicer*:

At the time we hired *S&S* as *our messenger service*, you assured me that you would provide prompt and efficient service for our company. However, since you began work for us, we have been extremely dissatisfied with the quality of your service. On several occasions, we received complaints *about packages delivered by your messengers arriving exceedingly late.*

I'm certain that you can understand that it is crucial for us to employ *a messenger service* upon whom we can rely. When you fail to live up to your duties, it reflects poorly on my company, and I cannot allow that. If we do not find immediate improvement in the quality of your services, we will be forced to take our business to a new agency.

I hope that won't be necessary and that you'll take measures to insure these problems do not recur.

Sincerely,

Graham Peters
President
LOST YOUR MARBLES TOYS & GAMES

THANK YOU FOR EFFICIENT SERVICE

Ms. Better Boxer
BETTY'S BOXES AND PAPER PRODUCTS
333 Main Street
Allentown, PA 12345

Dear *Ms. Boxer*:

It's easy to get so caught up in the activity of the workplace that you forget to tell people how much you value their work and support. That's why I wanted to make certain I took the time to let you know how much we at *LOST YOUR MARBLES TOYS & GAMES* appreciate the superior products and services you regularly provide for us.

As someone who also runs a small business, I can appreciate all the hard work it takes to keep customers satisfied. Throughout the course of our association, you have insured that *LOST YOUR MARBLES* always gets the products and services we need promptly and efficiently. Being able to rely on your efficiency is invaluable, as it enables us to better service our own customers.

Again, thank you for everything you do for *LOST YOUR MARBLES*. I'm looking forward to continuing a long and healthy relationship with you.

Sincerely,

Graham Peters
President
LOST YOUR MARBLES TOYS & GAMES

Consignment Agreement

Mr. Kevin Consign
KEVIN & KEVIN, INC.
500 Main Street
Providence, RI 12345

Dear *Mr. Consign*:

This letter is to reiterate the terms of our consignment agreement, as we determined in our meeting *earlier this week*.

According to our agreement:

(1) Kevin & Kevin will sell products manufactured by LOST YOUR MARBLES TOYS & GAMES on a consignment basis. LOST YOUR MARBLES TOYS & GAMES will retain the ownership of any and all products we manufacture.

(2) Any and all monies derived from the sales of those products will be paid to LOST YOUR MARBLES minus a percentage agreed on by both parties.

(3) Twice a year, an inventory will be taken of all products taken on consignment and sold.

(4) Either party may terminate this agreement at any time provided they give 30 days written notice.

Assuming that these terms agree with your understanding of our agreement, we will proceed with shipping you our products next month. However, should you have any question as to the details stipulated here, please respond in writing by the end of the week.

I look forward to a long and prosperous business association with *KEVIN & KEVIN.*

Sincerely,

Graham Peters
President
LOST YOUR MARBLES TOYS & GAMES

INVITATION
To Submit Proposal For Project

Mr. Paul Proposal
PROPOSAL AND SONS DESIGN
777 Park Avenue
New York, NY 12345

Dear *Mr. Proposal*:

We are currently looking to hire a firm to work on *a special project* we are currently undertaking. Having heard of your distinguished reputation in the business community, we would like to extend an invitation to you to submit a proposal for this *project*.

I am enclosing a description of *the project*, including our needs and expectations. Please put together a detailed proposal for this project, including relevant costs, figures, and timetables.

We need to receive your proposal by *the end of the month*. If you have any questions or need further information, please feel free to contact me.

Sincerely,

Graham Peters
President
LOST YOUR MARBLES TOYS & GAMES

ACCEPT PROPOSAL FOR PROJECT

Mr. Paul Proposal
PROPOSAL AND SONS DESIGN
777 Park Avenue
New York, NY 12345

Dear *Mr. Proposal*:

Thank you for your recent proposal to work on *our special project*. I am pleased to say that after a careful review of your proposal, we have decided to accept your bid.

As we outlined in our description of *the project*, we need you to begin work right away. I'd also like to set up a meeting with you to discuss the specifications of *this project* in more detail. I'll call you later this week to set up a time.

I'm looking forward to a successful completion of *this project*.

Sincerely,

Graham Peters
President
LOST YOUR MARBLES TOYS & GAMES

TURN DOWN
OF PROPOSAL FOR PROJECT

Ms. Margaret Loser
M.M.D. & O.
999 Greene Street
New York, NY 123

Dear *Ms. Loser*:

Thank you for your recent proposal to work on our special project. We received proposals from several extremely prominent and notable firms. After evaluating and comparing the many applications we received, we have decided to accept an offer from a different firm.

I assure you that your proposal was given serious and thoughtful consideration. However, we believe that the one we accepted was the one most suited to our needs.

Again, thank you for taking the time to bid for this project. Perhaps we will have the opportunity to work together on some other project in the near future.

Sincerely,

Graham Peters
President
LOST YOUR MARBLES TOYS & GAMES

PAYMENT ENCLOSED

Mr. Sam Supplier
PRETTY PAPER GOODS INC.
111 Mott Street
New York, NY 12345

Dear Mr. Supplier:

Enclosed please find a check in the amount of $542.75 in payment of
our May order. Please make a note in your records that our payment is
being made *within the 30-day grace period and that no finance charges
should be applied to our balance.*

*Assuming everything is in order, we will expect to receive our regular ship-
ment by the first of the month.* Thank you for your attention.

Sincerely,

Graham Peters
President
LOST YOUR MARBLES TOYS & GAMES
enc.

VI.

EMPLOYEE

RELATIONS

MEMO ON EMPLOYEE PROMOTION

IN-HOUSE MEMO

TO: All Employees
FROM: *Graham Peters*
DATE: *May 15, 1993*

RE: Employee Promotion

It is with great pleasure that I announce the promotion of *Ellen Employee* to *Sales Executive*. Ellen has been with LOST YOUR MARBLES for *two years*, during which time she has shown herself to be an exemplary employee and exceptional *sales person*. I am delighted to count her as a member of the LOST YOUR MARBLES team and am certain she will excel in her new capacity.

I hope you'll all join me in congratulating *Ellen* on her achievement and wishing her the best of luck with her new position.

MEMO ON NEW EMPLOYEE STARTING

IN-HOUSE MEMO

TO: All Employees
FROM: *Graham Peters*
DATE: *May 15, 1993*

RE: Welcome New Employee

I am pleased to announce that *Mr. Albert Sales* will be starting work today as an *Executive Assistant* in the *Sales Department*. I hope you'll all join me in welcoming him to *LOST YOUR MARBLES*.

Mr. Sales has an extensive amount of experience in the business and comes to us with the highest recommendations. I'm certain you'll find him to be a welcome addition to the *LOST YOUR MARBLES* staff.

MEMO ON EMPLOYEE LEAVING

IN-HOUSE MEMO

TO: All Employees
FROM: *Graham Peters*
DATE: *May 15, 1993*

RE: Departing Employee

It is with great regret that I announce that *Susan Employee* of the *Art* Department is departing *LOST YOUR MARBLES TOYS & GAMES*. *Susan* will leave next week to pursue other interests.

I'm certain you'll all join me in wishing her the best of luck in her future endeavors and letting her know how much she will be missed.

MEMO ON EMPLOYEE BIRTHDAY

IN-HOUSE MEMO

TO: All Employees   FROM: *Graham Peters, President*

DEPT: *Sales*   DATE: *May 15, 1993*

RE: Happy Birthday!

It's been my pleasure to count you as a member of the *LOST YOUR MARBLES* team. That's why it's also such a pleasure for me to be one of the first to wish you a very happy birthday.

I'm certain that your co-workers join me in extending you the best of wishes for a most memorable birthday. May it be the start of much success and happiness in the coming year.

MEMO ON EMPLOYEE RETIREMENT

TO: All Employees
FROM: *Graham Peters, President*
DATE: *May 15, 1993*

RE: *Wesley Worker* to Retire

After *20 years* of service to *LOST YOUR MARBLES TOYS &
GAMES*, *Wesley Worker* is going to be retiring. Throughout his many
years with us, he has been an important part of *LOST YOUR
MARBLES*. His hard work and dedication in the *sales department* have
been invaluable. I am proud to have been able to work with him.

While I am saddened at losing such a valued member of our team, I
am also gratified to know that *Wesley's* hard work will now pay off
and he will be able to enjoy and relax.

I hope you will all join me in congratulating *Wesley*. We all wish him
the best of luck.

MEMO OF
COMMENDATION TO EMPLOYEE

TO: *Esther Employee*   FROM: *Graham Peters, President*
DEPT: *Sales*   DATE: *May 15, 1993*

RE: Commendation

After reviewing the report on your annual employee evaluation, I want to tell you how impressed I am by your superior work habits and abilities.

You are to be particularly commended for the professionalism and expertise with which you conduct yourself at work. It is employees like you who give our company the fine reputation we have in the business community.

I want to encourage you to continue with these commendable work habits in the future. I assure you that your efforts do not go unnoticed, and that we all appreciate the hard work you've been doing.

Again, congratulations for an exemplary record. I am proud to have you here at *LOST YOUR MARBLES* and look forward to our continuing to work together in the days ahead.

FOLLOW-UP TO EMPLOYEE EVALUATION

IN-HOUSE MEMO

TO: *Irving Employee*   FROM: *Amy Andrews, Director*
DEPT: *Customer Service*   DEPT: *Personnel*

DATE: *July 1, 1993*

RE: 12-Month Evaluation

As you know, we recently completed your annual evaluation. After reviewing your record, talking with your superior, and meeting with you in person, we came to the following determinations:

Attendance: 7
Attitude: 4
Professional Demeanor: 4
Ability to Complete Work Duties: 7
Initiative: 3
Politeness: 5
Customer Relations: 5
Employee Interaction: 4
(on a scale from 1 to 10)

I hope you will take the time to review these findings carefully and to reflect upon your work habits. I would be happy to make an appointment to meet with you and discuss your evaluation in more detail.

WARNING ABOUT FREQUENT LATENESS/ABSENCE

IN-HOUSE MEMO

TO: *Eldin Employee*
DEPT: *Marketing*

FROM: *Amy Andrews, Director*
DEPT: *Personnel*

DATE: *July 1, 1993*

RE: Lateness/Absences

It has come to my attention that you have arrived late to work on several occasions. While there are times when coming to work a few minutes late is unavoidable, you have repeatedly arrived over twenty minutes late.

This kind of excessive tardiness is completely unacceptable; it is unfair to your fellow employees and also affects your ability to fulfill your duties. I urge you to take measures to insure that this problem does not recur.

I am expecting to see a marked improvement in your attendance beginning immediately.

WARNING ON POOR WORK HABITS

IN-HOUSE MEMO

TO: *Eldin Employee*   FROM; *Amy Andrews, Director*
DEPT: *Marketing*   DEPT: *Personnel*

DATE: *July 31, 1993*

RE: Improvement of Work Habits

Much of the success of *LOST YOUR MARBLES TOYS & GAMES*
lies in the consistently conscientious work habits of its employees. In
order for a small company like this to function efficiently, it is crucial
that each employee do his or her fair share.

In recent weeks, it has come to my attention that your work habits
have not been up to par. You have particularly been delinquent in the
following areas:

Excessive Lateness
Failure to Complete Projects on Time
Lack of Professionalism in Customer Interaction

I'm certain you can see why these habits pose a problem, and I hope
that you will take measures to improve in these areas. If you would
like to discuss this problem further, please feel free to make an appointment to talk in person. Otherwise, I expect to see immediate
improvement.

NOTICE OF TERMINATION
OF JOB—(NOTE: CONSULT WITH
ATTORNEY BEFORE USING)

IN-HOUSE MEMO

TO: *Eldin Employee*   FROM: *Amy Andrews, Director*
DEPT: *Marketing*   DEPT: *Personnel*

DATE: *November 1, 1993*

RE: Notice of Termination

As I told you in our previous conversations, your continued employment at this company was dependent upon your improving your job performance. Despite having received several warning notices detailing areas in which you were expected to improve, you have failed to make any significant changes in your work habits. We have therefore decided to terminate your employment at *LOST YOUR MARBLES*.

Please come to the personnel office some time today to discuss the terms of your termination and severance pay. I regret that circumstances have forced us to take this action.

NOTICE OF DISCHARGE
OF PROBLEM EMPLOYEE—
(NOTE: CONSULT WITH ATTORNEY
BEFORE SENDING)

IN-HOUSE MEMO

TO: *Eldin Employee*   FROM: *Amy Andrews, Director*
DEPT: *Marketing*   DEPT: *Personnel*

DATE: *May 15, 1993*

RE: Notice of Discharge

This letter is to reiterate the conversation we had today in the presence of *Mr. Esquire*, our company attorney. Due to your poor service record, *LOST YOUR MARBLES TOYS & GAMES* has decided to discharge you, effective *May 30*. This decision comes after several memos and meetings in which you were warned of the need to improve your work habits if you were to retain employment at this company.

To set down the terms for your discharge as we discussed them today with *Mr. Esquire:* in accordance with our company policy, you will receive severance pay in the amount of *one month's salary, to be paid upon your last day.*

I regret that the situation has brought us to this point.

NOTICE OF LAYOFF—
(NOTE: CONSULT ATTORNEY BEFORE USING)

IN-HOUSE MEMO

TO: *Wally Worker*   FROM: *Amy Andrews, Director*
DEPT: *Production*   DEPT: *Personnel*

DATE: *May 15, 1993*

RE: Notice of Layoff

Due to increasingly severe economic constraints, *LOST YOUR MARBLES* is being forced to cut down its number of employees. After a careful evaluation of our current organization, we have regrettably found it necessary to lay you off.

In accordance with our company policy, you can expect to receive severance pay. At your earliest convenience, please set up a meeting to discuss the specific terms of your severance.

If the situation changes at some point in the near future, your position will once again be offered to you. In the meantime, I will be happy to offer you whatever assistance I can in finding new employment.

I regret that circumstances have made this action necessary, and I wish you the best of luck in finding a new position.

Notice Of New Assignment
To Sales Rep.

IN-HOUSE MEMO

TO: *Susie Sales*   FROM: *Ben Boss, Vice President*
DEPT: *Sales*   DEPT: *Sales*

DATE: *July 15, 1993*

RE: Change in Sales Territory

Due to recent developments in our organization, particularly *the significant expansion of our customer base,* we have decided to make some changes in the sales territory assignments. I am pleased to announce that you have been reassigned to cover the *Northeast territory.* This new assignment will go into effect *at the end of the month.*

We'll be having a sales meeting to discuss these changes *on July 17* at *9 a.m.* In the meantime, you should familiarize yourself with the region and send out a letter to clients introducing yourself as their new representative.

If you have any questions about this change, please feel free to set up an appointment with my office to discuss them.

VII.

NOTICES AND

ANNOUNCEMENTS

NOTICE OF CHANGE OF ADDRESS

Dear Customers:

LOST YOUR MARBLES TOYS & GAMES is moving to a new home! Due to the rapid expansion in our customer base, we have been able to enlarge our operation significantly, requiring us to find larger accommodations. Our new space will enable us to provide even more products and special services for our customers.

Beginning *June 1*, we will be located at the following address:

LOST YOUR MARBLES TOYS & GAMES
111 First Avenue
New York, NY 12345

For your convenience, I'm enclosing a Rolodex card with our new address. And if you find yourself in our neighborhood, feel free to call ahead and set up a time to tour our new facilities. We'd love to have visitors.

Sincerely,

Graham Peters
President
LOST YOUR MARBLES TOYS & GAMES
enc.

Notice Opening New Location

Dear Valued Customers:

Due to the rapid rate with which our operation has been expanding, we are delighted to announce the opening of an additional location. This additional office site will make it even more convenient for you to take advantage of our many services and will help us more efficiently serve your needs.

On *July 1*, we will be opening offices at the following address:

888 86th Street
New York, NY 12345

The new location will house *our marketing and sales department*. Our main offices will still be the site of *our executive offices, as well as the accounting, legal, customer service, ordering, and distribution departments. All production will still take place at our factory space in New Jersey.*

For your convenience, we are enclosing a Rolodex card with the new address, as well as an updated telephone list, including numbers for employees and departments located at the new offices.

We all want to thank you for the support you've given that has helped us reach our current success.

Sincerely,

Graham Peters
President
LOST YOUR MARBLES TOYS & GAMES
enc.

NOTICE OF PRODUCT AVAILABILITY

Ms. Cyndi Client
President and Chief Executive Officer
CYNDI'S HUGGABLES & LOVABLES, INC.
444 Greene Street
New York, NY 12345

Dear *Ms. Client*:

Thank you for your recent order. Please note that the following products you requested are currently out of stock:

Sassy Sally Dolls
Wheels and Wagon Games
Dream Dolly House

We have put these items on back order and can ship them to you as soon as they become available, which should be sometime by the *end of the month*. Should you not want to wait, we can either provide you with alternate items at similar prices or refund a portion of your deposit.

Let me know how you would like us to proceed. I apologize for any inconvenience this may cause.

Sincerely,

Graham Peters
President
LOST YOUR MARBLES TOYS & GAMES

NOTICE OF DISCONTINUED PRODUCTS

Dear Valued Customers:

As part of our commitment to providing our customers with the most popular and innovative *toys* on the market, we regularly re-evaluate our product line. Due to decreased interest and demand, we have decided to discontinue manufacturing the following products:

Charlie Chess Set
Daffy Darts
Eager Egg Toss
Bible Action Figures

These changes will enable us to begin manufacturing some exciting new products we currently have in development. In the coming months, you can expect to receive some free samples in the mail, as well as an updated catalogue.

Should there be a renewed interest in any of the discontinued products, we will of course reintroduce it into our product line.

As always, thank you for your continued business and support.

Sincerely,

Graham Peters
President
LOST YOUR MARBLES TOYS & GAMES

NOTICE OF CHANGE IN CREDIT TERMS

Dear Credit Customers:

This letter is to inform you of a change in our credit policy. Effective *May 15, all overdue balances will be subject to a 20% finance charge.*

At the time your application for credit was accepted, we informed you that our terms were subject to change. *Over the course of the last few months, the number of our credit customers has increased significantly.* As a result, this new policy is necessary for us to continue providing products and services on credit *as it will enable us to maintain a steady influx of funds to cover the costs of the materials required in manufacturing products on credit.*

Should you have any questions regarding these new terms, please feel free to contact me. As always, thank you for your support and business.

Sincerely,

Graham Peters
President
LOST YOUR MARBLES TOYS & GAMES

NOTICE OF NEW SERVICE FEES

Dear Valued Customers:

Due to increasing economic constraints, we have been forced to re-evaluate our current operations. Our accountants have found that in order for us to continue providing the quality products and efficient services our customers have come to expect from us, it is necessary for us now to charge a small fee for certain services.

Please be advised that beginning on *May 15*, we will be charging an additional *$1.50 per carton for packaging of any products to be shipped by mail*. I hope you'll understand that this small fee will enable us to maintain our efficient services for you.

Feel free to contact me should you have any questions regarding this new policy.

Sincerely,

Graham Peters
President
LOST YOUR MARBLES TOYS & GAMES

NOTICE OF PRICE CHANGES

Dear Valued Customers:

In the past months, the costs of the materials and supplies used in the manufacturing of our products has increased significantly. As a result, we have been forced to raise the prices of certain items.

Enclosed you will find an updated price list and order form. I think you'll see that the changes are not significant. We have attempted to limit the increase by absorbing as much of the costs ourselves as we are able.

I'm certain you'll understand that this slight price increase is necessary to enable us to maintain the same high-quality products and services we have provided for you until now. Thank you for your understanding.

Sincerely,

Graham Peters
President
LOST YOUR MARBLES TOYS & GAMES
enc.

Notice Of Decrease In Prices

Dear Valued Customers:

As a result of significant changes in the costs of our materials and supplies, we are now happy to offer certain items at a reduced cost. Enclosed please find an updated order form listing the products now available at a lower price.

I cannot guarantee how long these lower prices will remain in effect, as the costs of our supplies frequently change. I therefore suggest you take advantage of these savings while they are currently available.

As always, thank you for your business and support.

Best wishes,

Graham Peters
President
LOST YOUR MARBLES TOYS & GAMES

enc.

Notice Missing Information On Order Form

Ms. *Cyndi Client*
President and Chief Executive Officer
CYNDI'S HUGGABLES & LOVABLES, INC.
444 Greene Street
New York, NY 12345

Dear *Ms. Client*:

When our ordering department attempted to process your recent order, dated *October 1*, we found that some important information was missing from the form, making it impossible to fill the order.

For your convenience, I am enclosing a copy of your order form with the missing information highlighted. Please fill in the relevant information and return the form to us. As soon as we receive the completed form, we will fill the order and deliver it to you without delay.

I apologize for any inconvenience this may cause you. However, we want to make certain our work meets with your exact specifications.

Sincerely,

Graham Peters
President
LOST YOUR MARBLES TOYS & GAMES

enc.

NOTICE ORDER IS READY

Mr. Toy Store
TOYS FOR TOTS
999 East 45th Street
New York, NY 12345

Dear *Mr. Store*:

This letter is to inform you that we have completed work on your recent order and it is now available for pick up.

You may pick up the order at our *downtown* offices, located at *888 Bleecker Street, New York, NY*, between the hours of *9 a.m.* and *5 p.m.* Go to *the Order Department, on the third floor,* and present your receipt. Please be advised that in order for you to receive your order, you will need to pay the balance of *$3,514.*

I am confident that our product will be to your liking. However, should there be any problem, please feel free to contact me. Thank you for your business.

Sincerely,

Graham Peters
President
LOST YOUR MARBLES TOYS & GAMES

Enclosed Is Information On Stockholders Meeting And Stockholders Proxy Form

Dear *LOST YOUR MARBLES TOYS & GAMES Stockholder:*

Another fiscal year is rapidly drawing to a close for *LOST YOUR MARBLES TOYS & GAMES*, which means that it's time for our annual stockholders' meeting. This year's meeting will be held on *September 1*, at *9 a.m.* at the *Bleecker Convention Center* in *New York City*. Enclosed, you'll find information on available transportation to the meeting as well as detailed directions by car and train.

We have several items on the agenda for the meeting, which you'll find on the enclosed schedule. I've also enclosed a shareholder's proxy form. Should you be unable to attend the meeting, your vote can still be counted by completing the proxy form and mailing it to us *by August 31.*

I look forward to either seeing you in person on *September 1st* or receiving your proxy by mail.

Sincerely,

Graham Peters
President
LOST YOUR MARBLES TOYS & GAMES

enc.

VIII.

MEETINGS AND

APPOINTMENTS

CONFIRMATION OF
OUR APPOINTMENT WITH YOU

Ms. Cyndi Client
President and Chief Executive Officer
CYNDI'S HUGGABLES & LOVABLES, INC.
444 Greene Street
New York, NY 12345

Dear *Ms. Client*:

I am writing to confirm my upcoming appointment with you, to be held on *May 15, 1993*, at *1 p.m.* in *your offices*. At this meeting, *I will be presenting my company's new line of toys for the fall season*. If you would like me to prepare anything in particular for the meeting, please let me know and I will be happy to do so.

Should you need to change this appointment for any reason, please notify my office and I will telephone to reschedule. In the meantime, I'm looking forward to our meeting on *May 15*.

Sincerely,

Graham Peters
President
LOST YOUR MARBLES TOYS & GAMES

REMINDER OF
YOUR APPOINTMENT WITH US

Ms. Ellen Advertiser
ADVERTISER & ADVERTISER ADVERTISING
666 Madison Avenue
New York, NY 12345

Dear *Ms. Advertiser*:

This letter is to remind you that we have a meeting scheduled for *May 15, 1993*, at *11 a.m.* to be held in *our offices*, at which time *you will present your proposal for an advertising campaign for LOST YOUR MARBLES TOYS & GAMES*.

Please telephone my office to confirm this appointment. Should you need to reschedule, I would appreciate your notifying my office as soon as possible.

I look forward to meeting you *on May 15*.

Sincerely,

Graham Peters
President
LOST YOUR MARBLES TOYS & GAMES

Follow-Up Letter To Meeting

Ms. Ellen Advertiser
ADVERTISER & ADVERTISER ADVERTISING
666 Madison Avenue
New York, NY 12345

Dear *Ms. Advertiser*:

It was a pleasure to meet you the other day and to hear your ideas. I appreciate all the time and effort you put into your presentation.

Choosing the right advertising agency for LOST YOUR MARBLES is a big decision. I'm certain you'll understand why I want to meet with several different agencies before making a final decision. However, I can tell you that I was extremely impressed by your ideas and that your agency is being given serious consideration.

You can expect to hear from me within the next several weeks with a definite answer. Again, thank you for your time and preparation.

Sincerely,

Graham Peters
President
LOST YOUR MARBLES TOYS & GAMES

UNABLE TO ATTEND SPECIAL EVENT

Mr. John Customer
JINGLE SPORTING GOODS
333 Wall Street
New Haven, CT 12345

Dear *Mr. Customer*:

Thank you for your recent invitation to attend *the Fifth Anniversary celebration for JINGLE SPORTING GOODS.*

Unfortunately, due to a previous commitment, I will be unable to attend. However, let me extend my heartfelt congratulations to you on this truly special occasion.

I hope you have a wonderful event.

Best wishes,

Graham Peters
President
LOST YOUR MARBLES TOYS & GAMES

AGREE TO ATTEND EVENT

Ms. Cyndi Client
President and Chief Executive Officer
CYNDI'S HUGGABLES & LOVABLES
444 Greene Street
New York, NY 12345

Dear *Ms. Client*:

Thank you for your recent invitation to *the celebration for the opening of your new store.* I will be delighted to attend.

It gives me great pleasure to be included in this truly special event. I look forward to seeing you at *the party.* In the meantime, please accept my heartfelt congratulations on this memorable occasion.

Best wishes,

Graham Peters
President
LOST YOUR MARBLES TOYS & GAMES

IX.

MISCELLANEOUS

MEMO TO
PROVIDE INFORMATION TO SUPERIOR

IN-HOUSE MEMO

TO: *Graham Peters*   FROM: *Martin Manager*
DEPT: *President*   DEPT: *Production*

DATE: *May 15, 1993*
RE: Requested Information

As you requested, I have compiled all the information we have available regarding *the projected costs and figures of manufacturing the Susan Sally product line.* For your convenience, I am attaching *several charts detailing all the relevant numbers and statistics.*

I believe the attached material is self-explanatory. However, should you have any questions or need any further information from myself or my department, I will of course be available at any time to assist you.

Memo to
Co-Worker Regarding Problem

IN-HOUSE MEMO

TO: *Wally Worker*   FROM: *Susie Sales*
DEPT: *Production*   DEPT: *Sales*

DATE: *May 25, 1993*
RE: Problem with *CYNDI'S HUGGABLES special order*

Last month I spoke to you at length about *the rather large special order I had received from my client, CYNDI'S HUGGABLES & LOVABLES.* At the time, you had assured me that *your department would be able to fill the order without any problem by the end of last month.* I was therefore extremely disturbed to find that *you had not even begun work on the order as of yesterday.*

Perhaps you did not realize that our customers depend upon receiving these special orders on time, and that our failure to fulfill our obligation to them causes a serious problem in our future relationship with them. I am now placed in the uncomfortable position of having to explain to our customer why she will not be able to receive her order by the date I had promised.

In the future, I hope you'll remember that it is extremely important that you *begin and complete these special orders on time.* In the event there is a problem *completing the order on time,* I must be notified about it as soon as possible so that I might *talk to the customer and try to assuage the damage.*

I would really appreciate your taking the extra effort in the future to guarantee that this kind of problem does not recur.

REQUEST INFORMATION
FOR TAX PURPOSES

Dear Customer or Supplier:

My accountant has informed me that, for tax purposes, we are in need of certain information from everyone with whom we have financial dealings. Please fill in the relevant information below and return this letter to me as soon as possible.

Social Security Number:
Federal Tax Identification Number:

Your prompt attention to this matter is much appreciated.

Sincerely,

Graham Peters
President
LOST YOUR MARBLES TOYS & GAMES

TURN DOWN OF REQUEST FOR CHARITABLE OR POLITICAL CONTRIBUTION

Ms. Philomena Parker
PIGEON RELIEF FUND
999 Park Avenue South
New York, NY 12345

Dear *Ms. Parker*:

We recently received your request for a charitable contribution from *LOST YOUR MARBLES TOYS & GAMES*. Unfortunately, we will be unable to make a donation to your organization at the present time.

We receive many such requests from many worthy and well-deserving organizations. I'm certain you can understand that it is impossible, particularly for a company of our size, to make a contribution to all of them. However, I wish you the best of luck in your fund-raising efforts.

Sincerely,

Graham Peters
President
LOST YOUR MARBLES TOYS & GAMES

AGREEMENT TO
CHARITABLE CONTRIBUTION

Mr. Phil Lanthropist
TOYS FOR UNDERPRIVILEGED TOTS
777 Golden Way
Portland, OR 12345

Dear Mr. Lanthropist:

We recently received your request for a charitable contribution to your organization. While we receive requests for donations from many organizations, all of us at *LOST YOUR MARBLES TOYS & GAMES* find *TOYS FOR UNDERPRIVILEGED TOTS* to be a particularly worthy cause. Given the nature of your organization, we are pleased to be able to make a donation.

Please find our charitable contribution enclosed. Additionally, should you be interested, we would be happy to *donate surplus and overstocked toys in the coming months.*

Best of luck in your most commendable endeavors.

Sincerely,

Graham Peters
President
LOST YOUR MARBLES TOYS & GAMES

enc.

INFORMATION ON FOREIGN SALES

M. Robert St. Pierre
LES TOTS
222 Montemart
Paris, France

Dear *M. St. Pierre*:

Thank you for your recent inquiry regarding foreign sales of our products. Our foreign distribution is not handled in our American sales office, but through an overseas distributor.

I have passed your inquiry along to their office and you should expect to hear from them shortly. For future reference, you might want to note their address and telephone number:

Mr. Johann Strauss
DAS TOYS IMPORTS
444 Krelig
Amsterdam, Holland

Again, thank you for your interest in *LOST YOUR MARBLES TOYS & GAMES*. If I can provide any more assistance, please feel free to contact me.

Sincerely,

Graham Peters
President
LOST YOUR MARBLES TOYS & GAMES